Quiet Retreat Teachings

Book I: To the Inner Kingdom

Diamond Mountain University Press

dmu-press.com

More by Geshe Michael Roach:

The Principal Teachings of Buddhism (author Je Tsongkapa, compiler Geshe Michael Roach)

Preparing for Tantra: The Mountain of Blessings (authors Je Tsong-kapa, Geshe Michael Roach, Lobsang Tharchin)

The Diamond Cutter:
The Buddha on Managing Your Business and Your Life

The Garden: A Parable

How Yoga Works: Healing Yourself and Others with the Yoga Sutra

The Essential Yoga Sutra: Ancient Wisdom for Your Yoga

The Tibetan Book of Yoga:
Ancient Buddhist Teachings on the Philosophy and Practice of Yoga

The Eastern Path to Heaven:
A Guide to Happiness from the Teachings of Jesus in Tibet

Karmic Management:
What Goes Around Comes Around in Your Business and Your Life

Quiet Retreat Teachings

To the Inner Kingdom

by Geshe Michael Roach

October 12 - 15, 2000
Diamond Mountain Retreat Center

St. David, Arizona

Diamond Mountain University Press

dmu-press.com

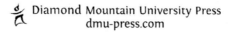 Diamond Mountain University Press
dmu-press.com

To the Inner Kingdom
Quiet Retreat Teachings
Book 1

Published in the United States by Diamond Mountain University Press
Visit our website at www.dmu-press.com

ISBN-10: 0-9837478-1-4

PRINTED IN THE UNITED STATES OF AMERICA

Book Design and Cover by Katey Fetchenhier

2 0 1 1 0 7 0 0 0 1

Table of Contents

Preface

We spend our days in gentle walks and thoughts
Of helping others, here in the silent
Peace of the forest, flowing in soft breezes;
We live doing as we please in our mansion
Of a wide flat rock, cool with the touch
Of moonlight and sandalwood scent of the holy,
Living deep within the woods
Of peacefulness, completely emptied
Of conflict and the afflictions.
– Master Shantideva 700 CE

Between March 3, 2000 and June 6, 2003, Geshe Michael Roach and several of his senior students engaged in a three-year silent meditation retreat in the desert wilderness of southeastern Arizona. During that time he didn't see anyone apart from the six retreatants, didn't get any news from the outside world, and didn't even hear the sound of a human voice. However, in order to fulfill a promise he had made to his students before he left, Geshe Michael came blindfolded to the edge of the retreat boundary twice a year to teach, and students came from Australia, Ireland, England, Germany, Mongolia, Singapore and throughout the United States to listen to these teachings.

On an isolated plateau at the foot of the Dragoon Mountains in southeastern Arizona, a long line of cars turns off the highway from Tombstone to snake their way across miles of dusty ranch roads straight into the desert wilderness. In the middle of nowhere we stop at a makeshift parking lot, and gather blankets, cushions, stadium chairs, water, food and extra clothing for the walk into a long, wide wash. Passing a tiny wood and canvas cooking yurt, we rush to find seats in front of a screened stage fashioned from plywood perched on top bales of straw and a framed-in screen with hanging sheets. Cows wander nearby, curious but not bold enough to approach.

Geshe Michael appears, blindfolded, along with the rest of the retreatants, so as to maintain their solitude. We see them emerging from behind some scrub mesquite, led by retreat helpers, and Geshe-hla takes his place in the center of the stage. The rest of the retreatants sit behind a screen so they can listen but not be seen. When Geshe Michael speaks, his voice hovers just above a whisper, raw from lack of use. He teachings feel directly connected to his wide open heart and mind, his speech washing over us in waves of wisdom and compassion. We feel he is pulling us in to briefly taste the profound experience of deep retreat. We laugh and cry, moved by the depth of what we are hearing and the intensity of the moment. During the break we pass around Oreo cookies and thermoses of hot tea.

As the teaching draws to a close, we huddle together under blankets, as the desert evening turns shockingly cold. When Geshe Michael is led off the stage we can see them disappearing into the brush by the moonlight, and someone starts up Neil Young's "Cowgirl in the Sand" over the PA system. Geshe Michael turns, laughs, and waves before disappearing back into a wilderness of cactus and mesquite.

These books are transcripts of those Arizona desert Quiet Retreat Teachings. It is incredibly rare to receive teachings from a Teacher immersed in deep retreat, and our intention is to share the special wisdom and blessings of these unique teachings with you. We have kept editing to a minimum in order to preserve the freshness of Geshe Michael's language and the several layers of meaning they sometimes convey.

First Day:

Thursday, October 12, 2000

I.

There be some standing here
Which shall not taste of death
Till they see the kingdom;
Jivan mukti, lu ma pangpar,
But how?

The choice is those you love
Ripped away, over the edge.
One house crumbles,
The other is sold.
The empty feeling of the unfulfilled,
Monotony to the grave.

You were not meant to lie within the egg;
Pierce the shell,
See the world color,
Fly to the empty sky.

Great Garuda,
Guardian of the children of the stars —
You will never be happy until this moment.

Now turn and see
Who put you here.

I haven't spoken for many months, so if my voice runs out, we'll ask Winston to help.

First I'd like to thank everyone for coming. When we are meditating, many times you come into the meditation, all of you, different people, and help us, like, "Wake up" [laughs], or, "Why are you daydreaming right now?" I'd like to thank you for that, and I know that it's because you're helping us and thinking of us.

Then, I'd like to thank the people who first brought us here from Phoenix, and the people who came the first few times to meet with the owners of this land. The owners have been so good to let us be here. We had many very wonderful times in their home, and the other partners too, who own this land. We met them and had very wonderful times together.

And then I have to thank all the people in New York who had many meetings and tried so hard to get it ready for us to be here. And then all the people in Mongolia who sent our homes here, and the people in San Diego who got them off the boat, and the people who drove them here, and the people who drove our things here, and the people who had the place ready for us here when we came.

When we first started, the yurts weren't ready, and we stayed in tents on the other side of the [National] Park. Every day we would wake up, and we could hear people working to put together some kind of yurt that they'd never heard of before. They didn't know which stick was up [laughs].

All day we heard them. At six in the morning we heard people; sometimes at eleven at night, we could hear people working to get our places ready, and it was very kind. And we'll never forget that.

And then when we came here, we were shocked that they were so beautiful inside. It's the most beautiful place we've ever lived in. Many people came to help, from many places. And then many people brought or sent things for us. People sent candles for light, and they built us beautiful altars, and people sent warm clothes and beautiful carpets to sit on, and many different things, bowls, everything we needed. People sent meditation cushions. People from all over sent everything we really ever needed.

We have a temple yurt, and beautiful things were sent for that, a beautiful statue of Lord Buddha, and pictures of many Holy Lamas.

That many people helped us. People came from many states and countries to work here. Also, the organizers, the director of Diamond Mountain and his family, and many other people have given up their lives as they knew them, to help us here.

Many people around the world, and in New York, took responsibility to take care of all the things, the projects we were working on: completely took responsibility. Local people from Tucson and from other places locally came to help build, to help us, to teach us about the desert. Some kind people took care of all the finances, sponsored everything.

We don't have one large sponsor, we have many small sponsors, helping as much as they can, and we know when we eat food that someone has paid for it. We know when we sit in our yurts that someone has paid for that, and we feel a very great debt, and gratitude to the people who have sponsored. There are many of them, from many places all over the world, who have sent what they could to help this place grow.

I think I'm probably forgetting something, but most important to us is, every day, we are given food. We hear footsteps outside, and sometimes on very, very hot days, they move very slowly, trudging against the sun. And then on cold days they move faster [laughs] and on rainy days they move really fast [laughs]. That's our caretakers.

These are people who gave up everything they had. They gave up their jobs—some of them had very good jobs—and they gave up the places where they lived, and they left their families. Some of them gave up all the money they had to help this place [cries]. They have brought us, I counted thousands of meals, always on time, always delicious, not just the taste, but the love. And so we'd like to thank them and the people who are helping them. They bring us everything we need. We ask; it comes. It's a strange world. Sometimes it comes just before we thought to ask.

3

It's an even stranger world. Thank you.

People spent many hours preparing books of prayers for us, thousands of Xeroxes. Some people prepared hundreds and hundreds of tapes of the teachings we received, and so we have everything we need. And, most importantly, I think, many great, dear Teachers [cries] and Lamas taught us what we needed to know to do this retreat for many years, from many places. They gave up their lives and their lifetime to teach us and other people. So we are very aware, and we think all the time that when we meditate for an hour, many people have spent hours of their own lives to give us this chance [cries].

I'd like also to thank all the people who worked to prepare this teaching place, and also everyone—the owners, and the rancher who has the cows here—have been very gracious and have respected our retreat boundaries very well, very strictly. We have had total quiet, except for Cow # 23 [laughs], but sometimes we need some fun. The caretakers and everyone have been very kind to make sure we're not disturbed at all. It's been totally quiet, totally peaceful here—outside [laughs].

I would like to also thank the other retreatants. They have courage. And in this life, in this world nowadays, it's hard to find something you can say is courage. They didn't know what was coming, and they trusted. They gave up their homes, they left their families—some of them have very, very close families, parents, sisters and brothers and boyfriends...and dog friends. It was very, very hard for them, and no one has complained, no one has ever expressed any kind of desire. I told them: "You can go anytime, if it gets hard for you." And they, like, laughed at me.

It's been very, very hard. The first few months we spent in tents. Some of these people had never lived outdoors, and they've had to deal. It was very hot in the tents, and then it started to snow [laughs]. And it was very, very hard. We were alone, each person. The nights are very dark, and there are many, many strange sounds.

One of the first nights we were here the first time, the coyotes came and sang to Pelma-hla, and she screamed. And the only person who came to help was Ora, who's almost as big as a coyote [laughs]. Every kind of creepy, crawly desert thing has crawled in people's yards and yurts, and sometimes very frightening things, but I think the hardest thing is the loneliness, to be alone for month after month.

4

We see each other for the holidays, like Sojong, confession ceremony, twice a month. When we're in deep retreat we don't see each other at all, so for a month or maybe two months. Each person has been very strong, become strong, and they showed a lot of courage, and respected the retreat boundaries. They've worked, very, very hard. They worked for, some of them years, to learn the meditations and visualizations that they have to do. We don't allow ourselves any other kind of stimulation, there's only meditation and some study of what to meditate about, and each person has done it very, very well.

They have translated, and are still working on great holy books about these meditations, some of them over two thousand years old. We feel constantly the lineage of the teachers [crying] from generation to generation who've taught these meditations. They are deep. They have learned very, very well, all of the needed things. So I would like to thank them for their example. I feel embarrassed to be afraid at night, if they're all sitting there in their yurts [laughs].

So we will have a small talk, and then a break, and then after that, maybe a short meditation. When the sun goes down the temperature drops. You might want to make sure you have something warm.

Before we came on retreat, my dear boss from many years of diamonds had us over for dinner, three of us, and he said, "Why are you doing this?" Everyone was stunned and it was silent [*laughs*]. But months later I thought of an answer [*laughs*].

Jesus was sitting with some of his disciples, and he turned to them and said: "Verily, I say to you, there are some standing here who will not taste of death before they see the Kingdom." "Verily, I say to you there are some standing here who will not taste of death before they see the Kingdom."
It means, you will pass into the kingdom of heaven before you die.

The Hindus call it *jivan mukti*. *Jivan* means while you are still alive, before you die. *Mukti* means freedom. The Tibetans call it *lu ma pangpar dakpa kachu du drowa*. *Lu ma pangpar* means before you lose this body, you will reach heaven, and that's why we came here. That's what we are doing, we are trying to reach this place [*cries*].

But there's no detail. Nobody says, "Now do this, now do that." The farther you

5

go, the less clear it is what to do. I think it's because so few people have gone there. Maybe you have to be a very special person to hear how to go there, exactly. So I would like to talk about this—how to go there, exactly, because that's why we are here. And there is no real choice, if you and I continue in this life in the way that we have.

I myself have seen so many people die. I made a list. I told Christie, "It will take a few minutes. It's probably only 10 or 15 people."

It was a hundred. In an hour. I was obsessed with it; I didn't know there were that many. And then I started to write down why they died, how they died.

Most of them didn't expect anything. Most of them didn't have much time to get ready. A very great number killed themselves, or abused themselves until it killed them. Very few left life happier then when they came. Almost none reached the theoretical average age. Some died before they were born. And it's only a kind of blindness that makes us look away, when another one dies.

In heaven there isn't this death.

We work so hard. I think we work hard because we don't want to think about what's coming, so we make little goals for ourselves: "I'll build a house for the children. I will reach a certain position." But it's just avoiding what's really coming. You don't know what to do, when you do think about it. That's why great holy beings have come to this earth to teach us, and a very lucky few people hear it.

I think the worst problem, maybe worse than death, is the simple boredom of this world. You can, you will—you do!—find things to keep you busy. You find challenges at work. You raise families that keep your mind occupied so you don't think about things. But really when you have time free to yourself, it's boring. You want something to do. You don't want to sit quiet and it's disturbing to know there's nothing very meaningful to do anyway.

As you get older, you start to realize that you will die, and I think that worse than the fear or the anxiety is the feeling that you were supposed to do something, and you haven't done it. You are losing the chance, because when you're old you can't move so well and your mind is slower.

So I think worse than death is the monotony, the over and over of life. And worse than the monotony is this feeling that you have left something very great undone that you could have done.

What I've seen here is that if you are forced into sitting quietly and thinking all day, it's exhausting. We go to bed totally exhausted. We fall into bed; I prostrate to my bed. You learn one thing—that there's very great potential in the mind. Your mind is incredible, powerful, beautiful, heavenly. On a scale with all the stars, of everything you can see, of all the planets you can imagine.

When it's dark here on the new moon, you see thousands and thousands of stars, and your mind is like that. You have some capacity there. Each person here, each living being, each of us has a mission to fulfill. There is a reason why you and I came to this world. There is something we have to do, and it is not just to eat, and shit, and die; that is not what we came here to do. It is not why we were put here. A normal person, and I don't know if there are any here….I mean, I don't know who you are. I can't see you. If I could see you, I still wouldn't know who you are in your mind. But if you are like me, then you're like an egg. You're like a small creature lying inside an egg. It's rare here to find eggs; the birds are few. There's not much water and they're small, but sometimes you find a beautiful shell of an egg.

Sometimes, sadly, you find an egg that fell, and you pick it up and you think, it makes you think, "What use is an egg?" If you're a vegetarian, especially. An egg, these little beautiful desert eggs, are something unfinished. They are like a Michelangelo sculpture that's not finished yet, and when you look at the egg, you know it's not what it's supposed to be yet. When you hold an egg in the palm of your hand, you know it's not what it's supposed to be yet, and each person is like that. We are not finished yet. It's important not to die before you're finished and become what you are supposed to become. Each human being on this planet is supposed to break out of that shell.

What is heaven like when you break your shell? What is it like? It's hard to think about heaven. It's hard to work to go there, if you don't know what you're working for.

Imagine a bird who breaks out of the shell and opens its eyes and sees color for the first time. Imagine seeing this world in black and white for many years, and

...hen suddenly you can see colors. How does a person who sees colors explain to a person who does not know what it's like—who only sees black and white? All they can say is, "there's something different, and it's infinitely more beautiful than what you know so far." And the black and white person says, "Tell me more," and the color person says, "It's hard."

The heaven has two parts. There's an outer, outside heaven and there's an inner heaven.

They are not what they sound like. When the bird breaks out, when you break out of your shell in this life, then you will see everything as heaven, and then you can fly. And seeing heaven is the outer heaven. Flying in the sky, being heaven, that is the inner heaven. Each person here must try to go there. It is why you are living. And you have even more to do after that.

There's a bird, Garuda, huge like a Phoenix, and it flies. It can fly anywhere; it's not bound by air. It can fly to stars....

Oh, I think we'll take a break. Please have something to drink, and talk quietly, and greet each other with big hugs, and rest. Then, when Winston makes noise like a Garuda [laughs], come back and we will have only a short meditation. Thank you.

Try to think of each person you met today, during the rains, and—I imagine—at the stupa in Tombstone, which is the Circle K. Maybe you met or saw some people there, and then on the road, you saw some people, and in your motel, you saw people. The people in tents didn't see many people, because they were trying to stay dry. Then, sitting in the sand, you have noticed the small desert creatures, which get bigger after dusk [laughing].

Imagine each living being that you've seen today. They are your children. Each one of them is your child. You don't become a child of a person by being born from them. They are your children since you were born here. That's why you were born here, to come and take care of your children. You will never be happy until you know this thing, and you start to take care of them.

Each living thing you met today, the rough cowboys in the Circle K and the little ants, each moving thing you saw today is your child by nature of things. You were

8

born here because you are supposed to take care of them. You are the one who is responsible for each of them.

Each person here, before their time is finished, will learn how to take care of every living thing they have ever met or will ever meet. You are their guardian, their parent, their mother. You will be the one who takes care of them completely, totally, until they reach heaven. You will be—each one of you—each one of us will be that one.

Oh, how can that be?

The world doesn't work the way it seems. You are not just another person living here. Events long before you were ever born were begun, were set in motion, to prepare you, to prepare for you. You, each person, before you're finished will become the single guardian, protector, and savior: the Jesus and the Buddha of each living thing you have ever encountered.

How can it be? There's not room for all these Jesuses on one world!

It *is* like that. After Jesus finished describing how to get to heaven, his disciples complained and said, "It's impossible." He said, "You're right, except for heaven, anything is possible."

In this case he is referring to what we call emptiness, the realm of emptiness. In the realm of emptiness, the ultimate kind of existence, in this realm all things are possible. You will become, you were meant to become, the one person who helps all your children. And when you, tonight, look up at the sky, at the dark, you see many, many worlds.

Out here, there's one beautiful thing with the stars. You can't go out to pee pee and look up and pretend this is the only world. It's not. There are many, many worlds. And you were meant not just to take care of your children in this world. Before you are finished, before events are done with you, you will and must become the person who takes care of living beings in many worlds: not just this one, but as many as there are.

You will become that; it is your destiny. It is what you were made for. It is why you are alive. You have a sense of that inside you, and you cannot be happy until you are finished. You will never be happy. You will never feel contented until you become what you sense you are supposed to become, and you will.

[Sound of planes overhead.] Those are protectors of the teachings; they fly over our retreat. There are no accidents. When a plane flies over, it's not a coincidence at that moment. It didn't just happen by accident. There's a reason for it. So look back through your whole life and try very hard to see how all the people around you your whole life have been trying so hard to bring you to what you must become. Each one was there for a reason. Each person you ever met was there to guide you closer to what you will become. Each person.

And then immediately you think of all the people who gave you trouble and say, "What about them?"

There's only two kinds of people: the ones who give you trouble and the ones who don't. And the ones who do give you trouble are also trying to get you somewhere. They were put there to bring you closer to what you will be.

So you can look back in your life. You can start with your holy parents and step-parents, and you can try to unravel the puzzle. It's like a game. What, what was that one trying to teach me? Why did that one hurt me? What had I learned from that? How am I closer to becoming the one who helps all my children in worlds—you cannot even imagine their colors and shapes and skies, what they are like.

There are no accidents, no mistakes, no meaningless events in your whole life. Each one was designed to bring you to what you must be, and you will be that. Don't wait. Don't think stupidly, "I can't do that; that's not for me, I'm not like that." You were made like that.

There's a part of you, inside of you, that will become that: each person, the protector of every living creature in their own universe. And you must fulfill what you were meant to fulfill. You will never stop, you will never be happy until you do, and in your heart you know that.

So I'd like to do a meditation. We will go for, oh, ten minutes, and then we'll stop for today. And I'd like you to do this meditation tomorrow, maybe once or twice before you come.

Go someplace, be quiet, by yourself, and go back in your life. Start with your parents, then go to your brothers and sisters. And then to the people who taught you when you were small. And then to all the people in your church or temple who taught you. And then all your friends. And then all the people you've met.

Pick the important, the big events of your life. Struggle to see how each one, even the bad ones and maybe especially the bad ones, was purposely designed to bring you here, and to bring you to the heaven.

We will talk more tomorrow about the heaven—what it's like, then a little bit about how to begin to enter it. And then the next day more about that. Then on the last day, we'll talk about the inner heaven, which is the heaven that when you reach it, when you enter it, you can finally fulfill what you are meant to fulfill by being here.

So meditate, now start chronologically in your life. What was this one trying to teach me? What did I learn from this one? And naturally, you will begin to feel grateful to each of them, even the bad ones. Especially the bad ones.

This feeling of being grateful is one of the most sweet meditations you can do, when you are feeling sad, when it's too hot or cold, when you feel sleepy meditating, when you can't concentrate, when someone hurts you, when you feel upset.

This meditation is so beautiful, and will always make you happy in a few minutes, because you can't ignore the fact that thousands and thousands of people have been kind to you your whole life. So start now. After the time is finished, I'll squeak some more, and then we'll go home.

[Silence as people meditate]

OK, so we started with something that Jesus said. He said, "Verily,"—that means I'm not b.s.ing you, in modern language—"there be some standing here which will not taste of death before they see the kingdom."

And then in the Hindu tradition called *jivan mukti* and in the Tibetan, the Buddhist tradition, called *lu ma pangpar*—before you give up this body.

Then we said that the idea is there, but it's not very clear how to do it. And then we started to talk about the choice you have. If you don't reach heaven in this life,

11

then you will slowly watch everyone around you die, like watching people ahead of you in a river go over the edge of a great waterfall to their death, one by one.

One house crumbles, which is your own body. The second house is sold. All those things you worked so hard for, for the children. And you know the children will sell them quickly and spend the money, and your whole life's effort, if that's all it was, will be wasted.

Then we spoke about that you have some potential. You will never be happy until you fulfill it. You sense something going on like that around you.

And then we said a little bit about how you are an unfinished product. You're not finished yet. If an angel were to come here and look at you, they would say, "Looks like an egg, not finished yet, didn't come out yet, just potential".

You have to see the world in color. Color means the outer kingdom of heaven. Then fly into the sky—this is the inner kingdom of heaven.

This is what you were meant to be. You never will feel happy, never will you ever feel satisfied, until you become the one person, in this world and many other worlds, who takes care of each living creature. You are, by right of your birth, the parent; they are your children.

You have to believe this. You were put here to be their mother or father. You were meant to do this. You know in your heart that it's true. You can't rest until you learn how to take care of each precious living thing around you, because you were meant to do that.

Then turn back and look who put you here. Events have been shaped. Events in your life have been molded to bring you to this moment. You were meant to do this. You must believe it and then you must do it.

Thank you again for coming so far, and thank you for taking care of us and giving us this precious chance, and we'll see you—oh, we won't see you—tomorrow [laughs].

Second Day:

Friday, October 13, 2000

II.

The kingdoms are two,
Inner and outer,
Come to the outer,
And then to the inner.

The outer is the apprentice song
The inner the air that carries it.

Both depend upon the fact
That nothing exists from its own side.

Make one decision,
Seek and learn
From friend and friends,
Hidden gems of the earth.

Samadhi is a state of grace
That borders on the Kingdom

Samadhi before the altar,
Samadhi before the world.

If you would be perfect,
Fight the good war
Against things:
Those that move and those that don't,

Advance guard and troops in the trenches.

Break the tyranny
Of the senses;
The devil is not gone,
Gone to the refrigerator,
The closet, the bed, the paper.

Behind the glass,
Behind the desk.
Seek first for the kingdom.

I'd like to meditate for a few minutes first. [Silence for meditation]

OK, we'll start.

First, one more time I'd like to thank all the people who worked so hard to make this place. We get up, well, we go to bed first, and everything around reminds us of other people's hard work to give us this chance.

Just pulling up the cover of the bed, there's something made by a Tibetan woman in India, and then you blow out the candle, and it's a beautiful candle that people have given us. And then you start your meditations as you go into sleep, and these are things that were taught by many wonderful lamas—especially a great one, the greatest one, in New Jersey.

And then sleep, and even in our dreams, people are coming often. And we see, not special things, but just people that we know. People who are here come often, and sometimes wonderful things happen in the dreams, and sometimes silly things.

Then you wake up, put your feet on the floor, and think about all the people who worked here. I look at the screws on the floor, and I think about the people I saw just before we started, working with these machines to put them together. They

14

were just normal people from everywhere, with no experience, but things came out so beautifully.

You can't imagine what it's like to wake up. You open your eyes, and there's a white round ceiling and spokes of a wheel colored with beautiful paint in Mongolia, and in the center, there's a hole with a design that looks like a cross inside of an eight-spoke wheel. They're very beautiful. The light doesn't come in through the windows, it comes in through the top and it looks like a cathedral all day.

Pelma is giggling about the rain that comes in [laughter]. It's a blessing. And then you see the altar. It's so beautiful. It was taken from a Christian church...with permission [laughter]. Then there are beautiful things—incense, everything we need, rugs made by Tibetans near the monastery, and more cushions than we can sit on.

Then we go outside, sit on the porch, look at the mountain and think about the owners of this property have been so kind to let us stay here. They're not asking for anything, they just thought it would be a blessing.

And then, I think of all the people who worked. Yesterday I forgot a few people. We have two doctors who are helping us. Sometimes we get a little bit sick, nothing serious, and there have been two wonderful doctors helping from different places.

There's one person who had a dental problem, and a very kind dentist came from Tucson and did work in the temple yurt with the person lying on the floor. Very nice—very. He doesn't know us; he just came, and he wouldn't take anything for payment [cries]. And sometimes we need books, special books, strange books, and we just write one of our friends in New Jersey or other place, and they come, right away, whatever we need.

And one big help we got was a person from Australia who flew here at his own expense and walked the property with us. He's a very great architect and he knows feng shui very well and helped us a lot. And he made beautiful plans for buildings that can be built here. And all at his own expense.

Many people like that spent many, many days of their lifetime, and again, we feel the responsibility knowing that you have traded your hours of your life for ours so that we can do this. And we try very hard not to waste the time.

Yesterday we spoke about why we came here, and we spoke about something Jesus said. "There be some standing here who shall not taste of death before they see the kingdom." And in Tibetan it's called *lu ma pangpar dakpa kachu du drowa*. In Sanskrit it's called *jivan mukti*. They all mean that in this life, the reason you came here is to reach a place—heaven, it's called in our language. And it's why you're here, to do that.

But it seems like sometimes there's not much detail about how to do it. So we started by looking at the choices. The choices are very simple. You just get older, and in the meantime you expend your life's energy. Some people faster, some people slower. You spend it on things that don't really mean much. And then you die. And you watch others go before you.

You don't have to live like that. If you can find that place that many great beings have come to this earth and described, then you don't have to live and die like that, without meaning.

The greatest meaning is not just to reach heaven; it's that in the last stage of coming into heaven you fulfill the reason why you were born. And in your heart, you know there is something you have to do here, which is more than what we see.

Each person here will "verily" become the protector, and the guardian, and the teacher and guide of countless other living creatures. You were born to be this. You will never be happy until you fulfill what you were meant to do, to take care of every other living thing in your world, and in all the worlds you can imagine. You are meant to; you were born to reach this place, and you will.

The heaven has two parts: one is called *chitab kachu*; one is called *nangitab kachu*. It means the outer heaven and the inner heaven.

First we come into the outer heaven, and then later you reach the inner heaven. It's always like that. You can think of the outer heaven as like a training ground for a student or an apprentice, like a musician. This is the outer heaven, where they are taught how to make the perfect song. You don't come into it in a day. It's a very gradual process, through hard work, and through knowing how to do it, through working hard to come there and stay there.

There was a big argument in Tibet. Some people said the outer heaven is a separate place. Some people said, "No, it's the house you live in." "Sera Monastery," they said, "is the outer heaven for those who know."

I think it's important to say there's a reason why there was confusion, why there was a debate between people who knew, who were there. Because if you look at it from one way, when you go there, it is where you were, but changed. And then on the other hand, it's changed so much, that maybe it's not the place you were before anymore. And that's why there was some confusion.

The outer heaven and the inner heaven depend on emptiness. Two people sit under this sun. One person is happy, they can get a tan. And the other person is miserable because they're getting sunburned. So how many suns are there? Is the sun that burned the one person the same sun that gave a tan to the second?

When you reach the outer heaven, you will start to see everything much differently. I think many people want to know if their loved ones will be there. They will be; they are there, but they aren't anything you can imagine right now. They're different, but they're there. You don't have to think or worry that it's like going up in the clouds and missing all your friends. It's not like that. There will still be those people around you, but they won't be in any way like what they were to you before. And they will teach you constantly, all the time, how to go on to the inner heaven.

And so it's like a circle within a circle. When you cross into the first circle, you have the great fortune of having many holy perfect beings around you helping you reach the inner heaven. And when you reach the inner heaven, you will be the protector and the teacher for every living being you can imagine around you.

And then some people ask, "What do those other perfect beings do? Retire?"—that's Rinpoche's expression.

The nature of emptiness is that you personally will be the one in your whole universe of all the things you see in the sky—of all the creatures that move on the surface of those planets—who protects them. The nature of emptiness is that you will personally be their protector. You will come to each planet in a way that helps those people.

And there are other beings doing the same in their own universes. How many suns are there? This is the nature; you can count on it. You have to fulfill why you came here.

So first you have to make a decision to try to reach these places. The books say you need renunciation. The books say you have to sit and think about how bad things are.

I don't know if you can do it by thinking. I think you need some kind of encounter with this kind of suffering life before you can really get serious. You have to have someone close to you die, you get terribly sick, you lose an eye, or you lose a brother, or something strong, your mother, has to happen. You don't make a conscious decision, I don't think. I think slowly you drift towards the understanding unspoken in your mind that you have do something to help, and then you start to look, and you have to find what's right for you.

The caretakers who take care of us and the people who help them—who are many, I think—they don't make one meal and split it up. They make one Caribbean rice and beans; they make one health food dish; they make an intermediate health food dish; then they make a dish for a very active person, and then they make, I don't know, Cheerios [*laughs*]. Sometimes, very rarely, they deliver the wrong basket, and we get rice and peas, and I think it's squash, but I never ate that much to know.

But it's amazing. The ways are like food. No two people will come exactly the same way. It's unreasonable to expect that of people who can't even eat the same food.

So we have to respect each different way. And you have to work very hard to find what's best for you, what food is tasty for you. You have to work hard to find the way. There are many different ways to go to the outer heaven and inner heavens. You have to find them and then work hard.

His Holiness the Dalai Lama [*Geshe-hla cries*] says that he's often frustrated with us because we expect everything very fast. It doesn't work like that. It's hard work. It's hours on the cushion. There's no substitute for it. You have to spend the time and work hard and know what to do. So you need a good teacher for the path that fits you, and you have to study from them. Then you need other friends.

I'm more and more aware that people like us don't learn from books, and we rarely learn from teaching. We learn from being around others. We pick up our traits from others we are exposed to and from media and other sources much more than from thinking or learning. We imitate; we emulate everything around us. And so you have to sift through the earth. It's like finding a diamond. Diamonds are rare because they're so hard to recognize. In a pile of regular pebbles, they usually look just like the rest, and then it takes experience and effort to withdraw the real diamond.

I think, as I get older, that the way to find a teacher is perhaps to look around you among the people you know. Choose the traits or qualities you would like to have, like honesty or the ability to be silent, or the ability to serve your teacher properly, or perhaps the ability to have the ultimate vision of life, or perhaps the ability to admit your mistakes, and to purify them. Among the people around you, there are those who have these qualities, each quality. I'm afraid there are people who I haven't recognized who have all of them at once. So I think it's important to find three or four very beautiful people, each one who has a quality which you don't have, and you know you don't have, and try to learn it from them through being around them, not from a book. These are real spiritual friends, and I urge you to try to recognize them. They may be old, young, big, small, any sex, color, race, anything. You don't know; it's irrelevant.

They could speak any language. They could be a scholar or a dishwasher in a small temple in New Jersey, but they have what we need, and they have shown those qualities. The way is to be near them, and study how they act, and try to be like them. It's much easier than a book.

I told you about the outer heaven, but not the inner. It's the difference between the medium and the message. It's the difference between a person using the World Wide Web, the internet, and being the internet. You send an email, and you are in a suffering world; you master the web, and you are in the outer heaven; you become the entire network of wires and computers that carry those messages of the entire planet, and you have reached the inner heaven. You become the entire network by which all things happen. And then naturally you are able to send messages any-where, because *you* are the web.

We'll say more, because that's not very clear, but it's true. Just a little about the outer heaven, and then I think we'll take a break.
How to get there…There are things you have to do in meditation, and there are

things you have to do out of meditation. There's a thing called samadhi. Samadhi is usually translated as meditation, but it is like a great plain that surrounds the kingdom of the outer and inner heaven. You must cross this plain before you can reach even the first heaven, which is the outer heaven. You must live on the plain for many weeks and months and years of samadhi. You have to learn samadhi first, before you can enter the outer heaven. There are no exceptions; you can't do it if you don't learn samadhi.

Samadhi is like a state of grace. It means to pass through the day, the whole day, in a state of perfect attention and peacefulness of mind. It's not the outer heaven, even it's mistaken for it because it's so beautiful, but you need it to come into the outer heaven. You need samadhi. You need this state of grace, this beautiful state of perfectly peaceful attention or focus constant throughout the day.

I don't mean to walk around like Einstein. It's more like to walk around in the state of mind you have when you're reading a great book, a novel, or listening to a great piece of music. You know which one I'm talking about. It's that state of mind all day, just imagine. That's why many people have mistaken it for heaven. But it's not heaven; it's a tool, and you must have it to reach the outer heaven. You will quickly reach the outer heaven if you have it. I'd like to talk about it and about some things we need to be in samadhi.

First one: I think about an incident that happened in Jesus' life. He was standing in the street, it seems, and a young man rushed up to him and said, "I want to know if there's a way not to die."

And Jesus said, "Keep the guidelines which Moses taught you. Respect life; don't kill. Respect other people's things; don't steal. Respect other people's wives and husbands; don't commit adultery. Always speak and live by the truth and by what you know is true; don't lie. Respect the father and mother who gave you this precious body to reach the inner and outer kingdoms." And lastly, he said, "Most importantly, treat other people exactly the way you treat yourself. With the same care and effort that you spend on feeding and caring for yourself, do it for others, with exactly the same effort."

And the young man said something surprising. He said, "I know those rules, and I have followed them my whole life, but still something's lacking."

20

And Jesus said, "One more thing, give up everything you have, and sell it. Give the money to poor people who need it, and follow me."

Why did he say that? It's because of things. If your mind is on your things, if you have invested your heart, your mind, and your spirit in things, then as Jesus says in the next line, your chances of reaching even the outer heaven are the same as the odds of putting a camel through the eye of a needle. You can't do it.

So the first thing to do if you want samadhi, which you must have sooner or later, is to fight against possessions. It's a war. They are sneaky. They sneak into your mind first. "I need this." And then they sneak into your house. And then, you used to have a big, clean, beautiful, white, sun drenched yurt and now it's a junk pile.

It's the things—they sneak in, and you have to be vigilant. You have to fight them. It seems funny, but it's true. The more objects you possess, the less samadhi you have.

There's no other way. You must take this to heart. You must fight them. Go home, pick up your broom, and beat them, push them out. "You go away, I want samadhi, not things."

Jesus says a beautiful thing. He says, "Invest in things that are endless. Don't invest in things that rust and that moths corrupt, in things that will just fall apart and you will lose."

There's nothing in your house that you need. We learned that when we came here. You don't need them. Even the innocent looking little extra books or furniture are your enemy. They are preventing you from reaching samadhi. They're not neutral. They are actively taking up part of your mind and your heart, and you can't think straight. You can't recognize the outer heaven because your mind is filled with knowing these things that you have.

You don't have to be greedy. You don't have to be attached to them. Their simple presence in your home prevents you from having samadhi. You have to remove them. You don't need them. You can live in a smaller place with an altar and a meditation seat, and a simple stool, and a few changes of clothing, and you don't need more than that. Then you can concentrate on reaching the heaven, the two heavens. Don't wait; just ask them to leave.

21

Ironically, I think that the people here who are most intelligent are most at risk, in the most danger. If they turn their minds to the collection of things, they are good at it. It's a challenge—how much money to collect or how many beautiful, tasteful, sophisticated things. It's those of you who are most talented, the most intelligent, who are in most danger from things. They will slowly take over your mind. Not that you are greedy or possessive. You are reasonable. They took over your mind very nicely. So you have to get rid of them. There's no choice. You need to reach samadhi. Get rid of them; they're like soldiers entrenched in your house.

"Not that one."

"Yes, that one." Just get rid of them.

"It's sort of lonely in a big house with no things."

Just get rid of them. Then deal with the advance soldiers, the ones that come into your mind and say, "I need just one more thing."

You don't really need it. We found that out when we came here. We lost almost everything we had, and we don't notice it at all. It's wonderful. Now there are new things attacking our yurts.

That's all. Be careful of things. What Jesus said is true. You can't have samadhi if you have many things.

There's a special case of people, though. I think of Lama Zopa, who uses many things well. These are very holy beings, who have the capacity more than we do to use many objects, because they're helping many, many people. They can maintain samadhi; we can't.

You should be honest with yourself, and remove things. Don't have things. Have only a few things that you really need and use, because you can't have samadhi if you have things.

Now, I ask you to take a break. Have some nice refreshments; I hope there's something here. Then when Winston makes some noise, please come back, and we'll finish quickly after that.

22

Again, samadhi is like a halo around your mind, the whole day. It's very, very beautiful way to live, and you have to have it to reach even the outer heaven, much less the inner.

The first enemy to it is things. The more things you have, the less samadhi you're capable of.

Second, we were born with wonderful senses, the ability to see and hear, smell and taste, to feel things. It's a great gift; it's a great tool. You will use them to help many beings, but they are also a great danger. If they are misused, they prevent you completely from samadhi; effectively preventing you from heaven, and from the higher being which you are destined to become.

The great Christian writer C.S. Lewis wrote a book called *Screwtape Letters*. We studied it in Sunday school. It's a book of advice from the Devil to his nephew, who has been assigned to corrupt a young man. And the Devil says, "One of our greatest achievements in the twentieth century is that people don't even believe in us. They don't recognize us anymore. We can live in their refrigerator, their closet, their bed, their newspaper. They don't even believe we're alive."

In the refrigerator is another great enemy to samadhi. Christie and I were sitting on the porch one day. We hadn't seen anything bigger than a lizard in a long time, and under the gate came a cat. We couldn't believe he was there; he couldn't we were there. He was a Siamese with beautiful eyes. I don't know how he got out here.

I don't know how he could live, but he was the most beautiful cat I've ever seen. He was shaped and he moved like a panther or a tiger. His body was completely different from other cats. And it dawned on me that every cat I had ever seen before that ate too much. He was beautiful. Then I thought, "I'm the same." We eat too much. You can't meditate properly if you eat too much, and what they taught you was enough is a lie.

The "food pyramid chart" of the United States Department of Agriculture was created by business people. I know. We used to do the same: "No man who loves his wife wouldn't buy her an anniversary diamond bracelet."

It's not true. You don't need three square meals. It's a mistake. You need two small, modest, healthy meals. And when you stomach feels a little full, stop. Even if the plate's not empty yet.

23

We can't do it. I can barely do it. It's a great test of will and strength to stop and not to eat all the altar cookies. It sounds funny, but it's deadly. The food will kill you. It kills many more people, I think, than people who starve. Food is only needed in very small amounts, maybe once every twelve hours. It disrupts the body. It's difficult for the body to turn it into the few tiny drops of essences that the inner body needs.

You have an outer body; you have an inner body. The inner body needs small tiny amount of essence of food. The outer body works for a whole day to distill into a few drops all the food you eat. And when you eat too much, everything is disrupted. Even when you eat a little, it's very difficult for your body to digest and to distill. When you eat too much, you hurt your strength and energy.

There's a beautiful passage in the Bible. A man is arguing with a disciple. Jesus comes up and says, "What's wrong?"

He says, "I asked them to remove a demon," meaning a mental affliction, "from my friend. They couldn't do it."

Jesus, of course, does it. The disciples complain, "You didn't teach us everything!"

He said, "This kind of demon needs prayer, meditation, and fasting."

You have to give your body a chance to rest. You will never reach the inner or outer heavens unless you eat wisely. It takes great skill and wisdom to eat wisely, properly. And then your meditations and prayers will be unbelievable. But we don't know, because we never ate that way. So, if you will be perfect, eat well. Take good care. Avoid the demon of eating more than you need to be healthy, and strong, and light to meditate.

Second, what the Tibetans call *to gu tam sum*. Clothes. Be careful; don't own too many. Own a few good friends that you like to wear, that are clean and that are pleasing to other people who look at you. And are warm or cool as you need. Throw out those you don't use. Don't keep too many. You don't need all the shoes you have. Get rid of things and you will come to samadhi.

Also, one great sense object is sex. We live in a country which has made it a god. You are trained indirectly from your youngest years to worship this god. You don't need it at all. It's another myth. You can be quite healthy and happy without it at all. In the meantime, take care. Enjoy, from time to time, properly, in the proper way with a proper person. And then as you move closer to samadhi, as you win the war against things, food, clothes, then gradually you simply won't want it much, and then not at all.

Then all of the icons of this god that have been built around you won't mean what they used to mean. You can admire beauty. You can honestly, frankly tell a person of the opposite sex, "You are very beautiful, you are very handsome," and not want them. And not want to use them.

This is in the world of samadhi. You can enjoy finally, peacefully, happily, other people, without using them. It's not that sex is an evil thing; it's a pleasant thing like eating. But as you move closer to heaven, you don't need food or sex or even your breath. You will change into something higher. In the meantime, be wise, be gentle, and enjoy. And then pray for a time when you will be freed from those obstacles of even needing or wanting those things.

Last thing, newspaper. I tell you honestly, from my own experience, that one five-minute perusal of the morning newspaper will destroy your samadhi for days. You don't need to know what the president ate last night or things like that. We are quite happy. We don't know anything.

It's not evil. The people who write the newspapers are honest, good people making a living. But it's a habit or a tradition that has grown up in our civilization, which is unnecessary and disturbing to your mind, eventually preventing you from having samadhi, and effectually blocking you from heaven. You can say it's a devil. I don't mean a guy with red horns and tail. Anything animate or inanimate which would block you from heaven is a devil, and they do exist. And the newspaper is like that.

Behind the glass of your television is the same. You don't need it at all. There's no benefit; there's nothing you need. It will disturb your samadhi. As you get stronger in your samadhi, and as you get closer to the outer heaven, television itself will change into something beautiful and amazing, and it will teach you. In the meantime, be careful. It's distracting. Try to just turn it off and see what happens after a week or two.

25

The last line of today's teaching means what I mentioned before. The people here who are most likely to be able to reach heaven, the intelligent, talented, well-thinking, logical, energetic people here are in most danger. They are in greatest risk of us all, because they could turn their talents to lesser things. Every great spiritual master who has come to this world has been challenged in the same way.

Lord Buddha could have become the emperor of the world he was destined to become. He refused. He went to the forest. Lord Atisha did the same. The very first words in the Bible from Jesus are the conversations in the desert with the Devil, who has offered him the world. And he says, "People need more than food to live. I choose the other."

So find an honest living—we need to have an honest income. But protect your samadhi; don't be trapped. When I made a list of a hundred friends, good dear friends who had died in my life, I saw that most of them had squandered this life on meaningless work. You don't have to live like that. This is a country blessed with wealth. You can eat a little; you can live in a small modest happy place quite well on a small modest job. And then, go home and do the important things.

Jesus says to his students—he's funny, he's sending them out to teach and to help people and he says—"I tell you, don't take anything. Don't take any money. Don't take a second pair of clothes. Don't take any possession, not even a staff in your hand. Just walk. You will earn your keep by trying to reach heaven." Things always come to people who are honestly trying to reach heaven.

Lord Buddha said, "Anyone who makes an honest effort to reach heaven will never want for something to eat or wear. I swear! And if it ever happens, I swear I will not be a Buddha anymore."

He said, and Jesus said the same thing, "Seek first for the kingdom. Don't worry where will I get something to wear? Where will I find food? Where will I find something to drink? Don't worry—it will come; it always comes."

The small things come, by the way, with the big things in the inner and in the outer heaven. You will have more than you ever dreamed of.

So we'll meditate for a few minutes. Not long, I know it's getting cool.

Yesterday, it was a meditation reviewing your life, trying to find the ways in which people are leading you. The world is sprinkled with divine beings; a certain number have been assigned to your case. And yesterday's meditation was to try to recognize who is suspicious—good person or bad person—who has taught you by being with you and doing what they did for you, beginning with your holy parents.

Today it's a similar meditation. We talked about lamas, friends, and teachers. I would like to do a meditation where you choose three qualities or traits which you find yourself frustrated to achieve. Perhaps it's speaking truthfully all the time. Perhaps it's admitting when you've made a mistake. Perhaps it's the ability to really dream and have a grand vision of who you will be, what you are. And then choose a person who has these qualities.

This is a free teacher, a free school—it's hard to find free schools. Find the person near you, maybe next to you, who has this quality and you know it. Then try to find three people like that, who you can teach you in their school of goodness just by being with them.

Meditate for about ten minutes. Choose three people who have the beautiful qualities that you find yourself frustrated trying to gain yourself. And then decide to try to stay near them and learn those qualities.

[The wind begins to pick up towards the end of the meditation session]

When you feel the wind come by you here, realize that it's a reflection of something inside you, deep inside you. There's a connection between your most subtle and second most subtle bodies and the wind itself. It will be important later, but you must have samadhi to learn about those things. And it's those things which will take you into the inner heaven.

Please practice those mediations again. The first one was going back in your life trying to identify people who may have been special beings trying to head you in a certain direction. The second one, now today, was just to meditate about three qualities that you would like to have and then connect them to three people you know. Then if you keep doing this meditation, you will slowly start to naturally spend more time with them.

Later you may recognize them as special too.

Third Day:

Saturday, October 14, 2000

III.

Whatsoever you would,
Move through lives
Without a ripple.

If you're not like him,
Judge not, for you will:
A plank and a piece of dust,
A mountain under forest,
For they are your perfect reflection.

Only a bubble
Touching a bubble;
Desert creatures
Fighting life
And granting it.
People and events

Live like the three,
Resist evil
First at the source;
But be gentle there as well.

Silence and a single point
Shifting throughout the day;
Hours on the cushion—
The outer kingdom's come.

In meditation one day, something occurred to me about gratitude for others, and this big idea came in my mind: if someone is kind to you once, you feel very grateful, and then, if they repeat it, the more often they repeat it, the less you feel grateful. And I was thinking that when we were in New York, if one of the caretakers had come and said, "I'm going to take a day off work and cook lunch for you," then you'd feel very honored. Then they come and say, "I'll take a thousand days off work, and I'll cook 10,000 meals," which is what they are doing, and even so, around meal number six you forget how much work it is, and how grateful you should be.

It's amazing, like that, someone says, "I will help at the center for a day," and you feel very grateful. Then if they move their whole family, everything they have, come to help their whole life, then you get used to it.

If a person says, "I will teach a class," you feel grateful. If a person says, "I will teach classes for years; I will take care of everything for years," then you quickly take them for granted. There are many cases like that. There are people here who gave much of their earnings for many years from working; they just gave it. The first few days you feel very grateful, and then you start to take them for granted. And other people give you the use of their land. The first day they tell you, you are very excited, and then after being on their land for a few days, you start to take them for granted.

There are even bigger cases, like with your parents where you don't even notice anymore how much kindness they have given you and continue to give you, because it's repeated over and over, so often. And with our great teachers, especially in New Jersey. You know, some lama comes to give one lecture, and you feel very grateful and interested. Then another lama spends twenty or thirty years every day teaching you, and after awhile, you just ask, "Why don't they give me a break?"

I think it's important, when you step on this land, every time you step out of your car, be like the pope, and kiss the ground, and think how many people worked to bring us here. Every day, over and over, the kindnesses become invisible, but the gratitude shouldn't.

So, starting from something that Jesus said. He said, "There be some standing here who shall not taste of death before they see the kingdom." And then we said that in the Hindu tradition, this is called *jivan mukti*. It means freedom before you die, heaven before you die. And in the Tibetan Buddhist tradition, and Indian Buddhist tradition, called *lu ma pangpar dakpa kachu du drowa,* to reach heaven before you give up this body.

And then we spoke about how maybe the details aren't so available, it seems. I think because so few humans who lived on this earth ever really tried to reach heaven, and then whatever instructions they left are by nature hard to find until you're very devoted to the search.

Then we spoke about the choice, which is continuing life like we have lived up to now: unhappy, unsatisfied, and as you start to get older, more and more pain in your body, parts of your body falling off or falling apart, and the pain of watching the people you love die, and knowing that even the youngest ones around us will follow in the same way. Then there's this feeling that comes to each of us at times, that we were meant for something better than this, something more than this. There's a bodily hunger that comes every few hours, for a cookie, and then there's an inner hunger that repeats itself from day to day. Consciously or subconsciously, you want something higher. You feel there is something higher, and it's a blessing just to hear someone say, "It's true, you were put here; you came here for a special reason."

It's the nature of all things, in an amazing way, that each of us is meant to be the teacher and protector, the guide of millions of living things. It is your destiny. It is what you will become inevitably, and it's a blessing just to hear it said out loud once in your lifetime. You will be the guardian of living things in many worlds before you are finished. Right now, you are unfinished, and you have to try to become a finished person. This is a great holy blessing to hear it said once.

Then we said the kingdom of heaven, or paradise, or *dakpa kachu* or whatever language it is, has two parts, the outer part, and the inner part. You reach the outer part first, and then you reach the inner part.

The outer part is like a training ground. You will meet many holy beings. They will guide you personally. They are guiding you now, but you don't know. Later in the outer heaven, you do know. They're guiding you to the inner heaven; your being changes completely, like the difference between birds and the sky. The outer heaven is like being a bird. The inner heaven is like becoming the sky and the most beautiful bird.

Then we said you have to make a decision in your life, before it's too late, to try seriously to find heaven. You have to find a teacher, and you have to start the long journey of recognizing all the teachers around you all day.

Then we spoke about a state of grace called samadhi. Usually it's translated as meditation, but it's more like a very wonderful state of holiness, and peace and focus all day long, even into your dreams. Samadhi is not the outer heaven, and certainly not the inner, but it's a state which borders on the kingdom. You must have samadhi to reach either kingdom.

We started to talk about ways to find samadhi, and the first one is to fight the war against things, the things in your life that draw your mind in so many different directions that you can't reach samadhi at the core. And we spoke about things in your house. It's not that you're greedy or possessive. You just have normal things in your house, but each one requires a small part of your attention. Its acquisition requires your attention. Its maintenance requires your attention. Its disposal requires more attention.

Things are a tremendous drain on your spiritual energy. You have to try to be very aggressive in removing them from your world, from your house, so you can concentrate on deeper things. Be aggressive and don't wait. Be radical in the war against them. Thrust them out of your house. Make a big pile for the garbage truck [*laughs*]. And then, beware when they start to sneak back in [*laughter*], and they will. A week after you throw them out, one by one, new things come to replace the old ones.

You have to try very diligently. Your life is at stake, and the lives of many other people. You have to try to act now while you're thinking about it. In the next week, remove most of the things that you have. You don't need them, and if you have all of those things, you can't reach samadhi. You cannot reach heaven. Jesus said the odds are like a camel going through the eye of a needle—and he wasn't exaggerating.

The second obstacle we said was the objects of your senses. You were born with beautiful eyes to see beautiful things, and enjoy them, and to hear beautiful sounds, and smell and taste and feel things. You should use those senses. When you have samadhi, they are heightened and stronger and you can enjoy things even more than before, but you have to rein them in. You have to control them. Once they

31

pass a line of moderate contentment, then they become chains and you become their slave. And then, your whole life is spent thinking about dinner, or thinking about boys and girls and thinking about clothes.

You have to remove them. You should eat wisely and moderately, feel light and strong. In the final stages before inner heaven, you will have to undertake very serious meditations, which cannot be done unless your body is healthy and strong and light. Then you have to be watchful of things that overload your senses, like newspapers and television. The mind cannot absorb so much meaningless trivia and still maintain samadhi. You have to try to avoid it.

The worst obstacle to samadhi in our lives is the urge to be busy, and to have many things happening, to be very busy at work. There are two reasons: one is that life is so empty that intelligent people find it more comfortable to be very busy, and then it doesn't face them starkly that life is so meaningless. Secondly, it's like a challenge. If you're intelligent, and if you're capable, if you are talented, then you feel challenged to try to do many great things that will crumble before you do.

It's much more difficult, and it takes a much higher degree of talent to conquer the inner world. A person who is really intelligent and talented should focus on the ultimate Mount Everest of your own mind, because the results of doing that remove the pain of countless people. And so, today, I'd like to talk a little bit about the inner causes of samadhi. Food, clothes, and the things in your house are outside of you, but there are things inside that you need for samadhi.

There's one inside thing, which is very helpful for samadhi, for this blessed state of grace, for this beautiful halo around your mind all day. It's very unexpected. It's simply being considerate of other people, to think about them.

You go to the bathroom, and it's late at night, and you know that if you flush the toilet it might wake someone else. So you wait, or you hold it all night, and this is a kind of what they call in Tibetan *dakshen nyamje*. You're exchanging your happiness for that of others. Out of consideration of how others will feel, you refrain from doing something.

In the Abhidharma, *ngotsa yupa* and *trel yupa* are the two mental states which accompany all goodness—worrying about how others might be affected by what you do, worrying about what they might think. If you can develop this kind of daily behavior, then samadhi is yours; it comes. It's unexpected but it's true. "What-soever you would have men do to you, do you even so to them." This is the law. This is everything.

Then, the main inner cause for samadhi, the way to reach samadhi, and the main key to the outer heaven, is very difficult. It's not judging other people, to not judge others. The Lord Buddha said, in a very heartbreaking talk, *"Nga am nga dang drawe gangsak gi tsu sung gi, gang sak gi gang sak gi tsu sungwar mi ja te, nyam-par gyur ta re."* If you're not like me, if you don't have the ability to read another person's mind directly, then please don't judge others, you will suffer.

He said that after telling a long sad story about a person who had judged another monk wrongly and then had suffered for thousands of years, and at the end of the story, he reveals that he was the person who made the mistake.

Jesus said the same, "Judge not, lest you be judged."

I was thinking, you don't very often find cases in the books where these beings make a joke, and I was curious, because the great beings of our times, His Holi-ness the Dalai Lama, Khen Rinpoche Geshe Lobsang Tharchin, matchless one, and Lama Zopa are funny sometimes [*laughs*]. Then I read where Jesus said, "You have a plank in your eye, and you complain about a mote of dust in your brother's eye."

I think in modern language, it would be like, "You've got a two by four sticking out of your eyeball, and you're worrying about a piece of dust in your friend's eye. Don't worry about the piece of dust, take care of the two by four in your eye first" [*laughs*].

I think there are deeper reasons why Jesus was talking about eyes. He didn't say you have a big stick coming out of your back or your arm. He said your eye. Why did he say your eye? Many reasons. The most important is that as you judge oth-ers negatively, then each time you judge them, "I think this person is doing this bad thing. I think this person is stupid. I think this person doesn't look so nice." Every single time a single thought like that crosses your mind, which is hundreds of times in an hour, each time a very powerful seed is planted within your own mind. That seed will cause you to see a stupid person, and a bad person, and an ugly person again, many, many times. Imagine—this happens every time we think we know another person's thoughts, every time that we think we know why they're acting in a certain way. Each time you see evil around you, you plant a seed in your own mind to see it again, and again, and again.

It's important to realize that reality is a perception, only a perception. If you think carefully, you can grasp that everything you see is only random colors and shapes. There must be something in your own mind which is causing you to see those random colors and shapes as people, or sky or sun or land or stupid people or bad people or ugly people. It isn't coming from them at all.

Not one iota of evil around you on a personal level, on a national level, on a global level, not one negative thing that you experience exists from its side. It is seen by you with your two by four eye because of a seed in your own mind. As you walk across this desert, as you drive here, as you interact with the other people here, you are experiencing a perfect mirror reflection of your own soul.

It's frightening. Every bad thing you ever saw with two by four eyes was your own two by four. Nothing exists from the other side, so when you judge it, when you complain, when you feel revulsion for another person, you are really just deeper in the same mire. You will see it more and more.

It's not on a psychological level. It's not that people who had a good breakfast see the world better. They do. I'm not talking about that kind of subjectivity. I'm talking about your mind shaping the detail of every object around you, even those objects. You cannot see a bad person unless you have been one. You are seeing your own reflection, and when you judge another person, it becomes worse. You are assuring that you will continue to see them in the future.

So if you would enter the outer heaven, you must realize this one thing and act on it. Keep your mind in a state of suspension. This person seems to be doing something wrong, evil, but I don't know for sure. I can't read their mind. Let me keep my mind free of assuming anything about them. I think you will quickly see them change.

I was sitting with Christie meditating. We have a dome over the yurt. There's a big hole, and beautiful sunlight and stars come through, and the moon. There's a screen, and on the screen there lives a big fat lizard. He gets fatter all the time than the other lizards, because flies like the dome.

34

There's another lizard that lives in the yurt, has been there from the beginning. He first, I think it was him, came on the altar and draped himself over Vajrayogini's shoulders, and refused to move. I think of him as "junior" because he's always around. He sometimes sits on your knee when you meditate.

In deep meditation, you stare at the dome, trying to go back to meditation, and one day there was a ruckus on the screen which is a big event for us [*laughter*], and there was a little tiny lizard, very, very beautiful. He has a big head like a puppy and a tiny little body. He's about an inch long or inch and a half and the big lizard would chase him to the other side of the screen, and he would run faster. And it looked like a horse race, and it was great fun to watch. For people like us, this is a big event [*laughter*].

So, after a few days, we noticed that the little one hasn't come out. He sleeps over a piece of tape on the screen, and he didn't move, and suddenly I realized he might be stuck on the tape. I reached up and pulled down the tape. It's heavy duct tape, and he was stuck on the tape. This tiny beautiful creature, his fingers are like tiny spider-web needles, long, beautiful, and he was completely stuck on the tape.

When you're meditating all day, everything is much more powerful, and it seemed like the end of life itself. And here are two huge humans looming over a piece of tape with a small creature flailing on the tape and can't get himself off. She tried to pull his hand off the tape, and the fingers started to rip [*tears in voice*]. She tried to help him, and his throat broke open. A small drop of blood came out, and I thought, "This is a lot of blood for him."

I ran to get some alcohol or solvent, and then I stood over him thinking, "If I put it on him, it might kill him, but if I don't, he's going to die anyway."

And so we did, and he came off. He moved a little bit, and then we set him in the sunlight on some wool, and there was nothing else to do. We tried to meditate, but you can't and you're checking to see, and he started to move, and we were very happy.

Then I started to think, when I was watching him flail, that I can't tell him I'm trying to save his life. He won't understand. There's no way I can tell him, "Don't put your tail back on the tape. I just got it off." You know, "Hold still, be patient. It hurts; it's part of something bigger."

Then it dawned on me that there are beings all around us, constantly, trying in the same way. There must be higher beings. It's naïve to think we are the only level of things. We look like little lizards to them. We flail when they try to help us. We think, "They're trying to kill me."

You can't judge events more than people. Events could be designed to strengthen and prepare you for something higher that is so foreign to you that you can in no way be communicated with by those beings, any more than a small lizard can be told to lie still.

All events are like this. Negative things that happen to you, in addition to negative people you meet are certainly something of a larger master plan for you. You have to try to be still, and not fight too much against those who are trying to save your life, even if it hurts.

He crawled to the corner of a woolen shawl, and after a while he was very still, still for a long time. Then a fly came and landed on him, and Christie said, "I think he's dead. He must be dead." He didn't even move for his food. His food is going to eat him now. It really felt terrible.

And the lizard that lives in the yurt, strangely ran to the scarf. He chased the fly away, and he stood before the smaller lizard like a great God up on his legs, which they rarely do. He looked like a supreme being for a moment, and I thought, "It looks like he wants to bring him back to life. It would be so wonderful if he had the power."

We kept meditating, and when we looked up—you know the end of the story — he was running around very happily.

It was a very eerie feeling to judge another being as a lower, stupid form of life that hangs around the yurt, looking for stray flies, and then for a few moments, to entertain the possibility that this is a divine being. We are like bubbles. We have huge bubbles surrounding us, which is our world, our perceptions, our experiences. Sometimes the two bubbles meet, like helmets, like space helmets, and at that one point of contact, you experience another person or living thing.

Based on the one tiny patch of contact, you make an assumption about their whole life, their whole being, everything they know and are. You see a tiny, tiny spot of

36

their bubble, and then you assume they are what you think. You are really only seeing a piece of your own bubble.

It's completely true that that lizard wasn't anything from his own side. If I have goodness in my heart, if I have a great deal of goodness in my mind, I would certainly experience him as a towering angel, giving off light, come to guard me and my yurt while I meditate.

It's not an exaggeration. You have to understand. He is one more color and shape. My mind is making him an object. My mind, according to its goodness, is making me see something. It, my mind, is organizing that color into a lizard. There is no lizard. There's only colors and shapes. If my mind were more pure, if I had not judged others constantly through my whole life, then I would have the fortune to see a divine being. I would have entered a part of the outer kingdom.

So I think we have to be like Gandhi said. He had his favorite three monkeys and I grew up seeing this picture from time to time thinking it was just sort of funny. There's one monkey holding his hands over his eyes and there's another monkey holding his hands over his ears and the third monkey holding his hands over his mouth. We have to be like those monkeys refusing to see evil.
If you think you see evil then reflect on where it is coming from and reflect on the fact that you are like the little lizard. You can't tell what's happening really. Don't hear evil when people speak. If someone says something horrid to you—let it go. Don't think of them as bad because then they will become bad. When you think of them as bad you plant a seed in your mind to see them as bad. They're bad because you're bad. Not because they're bad.

Lastly don't say anything, don't speak evil. Don't let yourself think evil or speak it to others because it will become evil.

Last thing, then we take a break.

So if I see someone hurting someone else, should I just put my hands on my eyes, and not help them? Resist evil on two fronts. First, resist evil from the place where it came from. When you see a person hurting another person, it is only because you have hurt people. You can't see it if you don't have it in you. It's more than that. You see it *only* because you have it in you. If you have a person close to you who is jealous constantly then the best way, the only real way, to resist evil is to root out the seeds of jealousy in your own mind. Then you won't see that—it will change. It does not change by talking to them or fighting with them. It only changes if you can remove the seeds of jealousy in your own heart.

I'm not talking about a naïve ignoring of the evils of the world. I'm talking about a radical attempt to remove them, eradicate them from their root permanently. It's not that that person continues to be jealous and you refuse to see it. It's that they are no longer jealous—because you cannot see it, because you have removed it from your own heart. This is the way to resist evil at its source.

[Break]

So to repeat, the world around you, all the colors and shapes and sounds, from their own side, are random. They don't make any sense. They are just kinds of energy aimed at you. Your mind organizes the colors—neutral colors, shapes, and sounds into objects, ultimately into people, even yourself, and it does so under the influence, or even dictated by, seeds which you have put in your own mind before.

It means every negative event or person you have ever experienced, directly or by hearing about it, was created by your mind. It's a reason not to judge others. It's a reason to pull the two by four out of your eye first, and then you'll be able to see that these beings are trying to save you, and you will enter the outer kingdom. So you are the source of all evil and that means you can be the one to end all evil. You can, in this way, become the guardian of countless beings. This is the key to why you personally can become the single one who brings comfort and happiness to every being in your world. So be gentle when you think of yourself as having caused all this trouble, because you will be the one to stop it.

And the last thing I'd like to say about samadhi is to be gentle with yourself in many ways. Sleep enough. This is very important for samadhi. When you are tired, when you haven't slept properly as you need to, then samadhi goes away and everything gets bleak and you can't see holy things around you. So be gentle, take good care of your health. If you need to, then do some kind of exercise. It is good for your heart and mind, and in the end it is very good for your deep meditations, to enter the inner kingdom, which requires great strength and perseverance, and good health.

Lastly, take breaks when you need them. All great religions have special times of the year when people relax. You eat too much happily, and it's a goodness. You play at games and don't worry about meditation, et cetera for a few days. In Tibet, this is Munlam Chenmo, instituted by the matchless savior Je Tsongkapa. In the monasteries, it's called *gak-ye*. After a strict period of meditation, then have three weeks of any kind of game, or playing music, or resting. Your mind needs that. It's good for your samadhi.

Samadhi, when you reach it, is a state of mind that you can keep all day long. It is characterized by a kind of inner silence, and if you can maintain an outer silence as much as practical in your circumstances, this is very good for samadhi—to be alone, to be quiet, to be silent. It's good for people who want to reach this kingdom to learn to be comfortable with each other in silence.

We live in a culture where we feel most comfortable talking constantly, even if there's not much to say. But if you can learn the art, and if you can try to be with friends who understand the benefit of contented silence, being with one another, in love, and silent, is a great blessing and benefit for samadhi.

The main characteristic of samadhi is to be silent, and to be totally aware, totally into the present moment. It doesn't mean you don't plan for winter, for example. It means, when you plan, plan single-pointedly. You concentrate on what you're doing, even if what you're doing is for the future. You are in the present thinking about the future.

At all times be happy, be contented, be strong enough to be in the present moment: aware, deeply aware of what you're doing in the present moment. Surrender yourself to this moment. Concentrate on the divine things happening to you in this one moment, and don't be distracted by the future or the past. Future things, worries, anxieties, plans, and past memories, friends, things you used to have, these are very similar to having too many things in your house. They have the same effect on your samadhi.

To constantly think about the past, to constantly think about tomorrow, or after what you're doing now, is a great obstacle to samadhi. Be deeply concentrated on what you're doing at this moment, and then shift the concentration to the next thing you're doing. There is no clear border drawn by your activities, because the samadhi flows from the first activity to the second, steadily. There is no beginning of one activity, and no clear-cut end and then beginning of the next. You are flowing from one to the next in perfect concentration. If the concentration wavers, stop, rest, and bring your mind to the present. This is a way to enter the outer kingdom.

All of what we've said so far about samadhi is outside of meditation. Now let's talk about samadhi in the meditation. There's only one line in your text about meditation sitting on your cushion, and it says, "Hours on the cushion," In Sanskrit: *sa tu dirghakala nairantarya satkara asevitah drdhabhumih.* A very beautiful line. *Sa tu* means "about [meditation]," *dirghakala,* "unfortunately, there's no substitute for long hours on the cushion," *nairantarya,* "uninterrupted flow of practice."

Never miss a single day of meditation, one to three hours per day in deep meditation. Uninterrupted flow, every single day. I have in my old age understood that if you do anything for about an hour and a half a day, you get good at it. Eating or sleeping or meditating, and later you start to really like it. There's no substitute.

Satkara must be done properly. You have to know what you're doing. If you can get good instruction from a person who not only knows about meditation, but who meditates well, and who meditates *dirghakala nairantarya satkara,* then you can save yourself years of trouble and mistakes. One serious mistake in meditation will make it no fun. You will waste your time; you will give it up. So, *satkara,* find a good person who is really a good meditator and have them help you do it the right way.

Asevitah, "you must cultivate it like a garden," from week to week, month to month. If you never miss a day you will become a great master of meditation. You can start to see things that you never imagined. You can enter the outer heaven. It can't happen if you don't do it regularly.

Every day, with no breaks, properly, *satkara,* right way. Then *drdhabhumi,* "it will become strong, you will become good at it." You will start to like it more and more. Instead of making excuses not to meditate you will make excuses to go meditate.

There's nothing else to say about meditation except that you have to do it. The books in Tibet about the most advanced states of meditation, dzok-rim—we will speak a little about tomorrow—are very frustrating in a way, because it's clear that you can't explain many things to another person about it unless they are meditating a lot regularly, and so they can't be communicated to you.

It's like trying to speak to the little lizard, "Don't thrash around; try to be still." The gap is too far between, to describe many things, so *dirghakala*, be patient. It takes hard work for a long time. It doesn't happen overnight. Let's be honest. It takes months and years to get really good at it. *Nairantarya*, don't ever miss a day. *Satkara*, do it properly. *Asevitah*, take the time and the love of others.

You can't help them; you can't enter the inner kingdom especially until you're good at meditating. Keep others in mind. Maybe if you have someone who died close to you, then remember them when you're tired, or you don't feel like meditating, you have to help them. You should try. It's better to sit tired, for an hour, and not do very well, than to break your discipline, and it takes discipline, or you won't be able to reach the inner heaven especially.

Today we spoke first about inner aid to samadhi. Think about others. Wash the dish in the sink, clean the toilet if it's dirty, before you leave. Don't make noise if someone's sleeping.

These are small things. They directly help huge samadhi. Most importantly, don't judge others around you. There are events of galactic magnitude taking place around you. There are no accidents. There are no coincidences. There is a constant striving of innumerable holy beings to attempt to bring you personally to your destiny at every moment. Don't think less than that. Don't judge small events in a small way. They are all aimed at bringing you personally to fulfill why you came to this life. See you tomorrow.

Fourth Day:

Sunday, October 15, 2000

IV.

To learn to play
The final song
You must become then
Sound itself:
Enter the inner kingdom.

The breath, the wind, the inner wind
Moving in reflection
Of heart and understanding,
Key to the realm of emptiness,
Key to the impossible
Possible for heaven,
For in this realm believing
Becomes reality.

Nothing greater than these two;
You have spoken true, and you
Are not far from the Kingdom.

I was thinking that when someone starts a project like three year retreat, then many people pop up at the beginning, and they're very excited. Everyone says, "I'll pitch in and I'll do something." Some people come and say, "I'll do the three year retreat." Then others say they'll help. In Tibetan, it's called "ep tsar sap". That means the novelty of the thing, and usually, you know, it wears off. People often aren't able to do what they hoped. But this has been different.

The people who said they would come and do retreat on March third walked over the border of the retreat on March third, and when the time came, they undertook perfectly all the responsibilities of a retreat. They haven't broken silence since we began here in this area, about two months after we started, after training was finished. They've been very strict: we don't count laughing [laughing].
There's a true story of two people sitting on the ground eating and a seven foot scarlet snake raised its head over one of their shoulders, and the other said "Come," [laughing]. They don't bite. He didn't come, he went away.

But aside from emergencies like that, people have been extraordinarily disciplined. No one has left the "tsam." "Tsam" means border of the retreat, and very few people have entered. The retreaters have been subjected to terrible heat, and extreme cold. They've had terrible wind storms here, there have been many encounters with wild animals, some very dangerous.

I think most difficult is all the doubts and anxieties and the worries about the past and future that anyone would have, and missing their families and other loved ones. But they have persevered and worked very hard. They meditate many hours a day. They have a very strict schedule of study. They're working hard to translate many books, many ancient books of instruction for people who come later. They have written down the very beautiful and difficult instructions for all the meditations and special ceremonies that we were taught. They have done very, really well, and been very brave.

We don't see anyone; they don't see even the caretakers. We haven't seen them since March third. They pass the food through a special box, and so the biggest difficulty, I think, is loneliness. Each of them has dealt with it very bravely and become very strong, I think.

They also each undertook some kind of physical exercise to help in meditation. We have very kind teachers of different traditional methods, who have trained us and who continue to come without asking for anything, to help during special periods when we're allowed to do that. We don't have any correspondence. Occasionally we write a letter to the caretakers asking for toilet paper, and other important things. And we have no stimulation. The people in retreat have no other books, no other things, we just meditate.

The three caretaker people especially—and the people who help them—sincerely offered to take care of us without pay and they left everything they had. They not only cook, they clean. And when something flies off a yurt in a wind storm, they come with hammers and fix it.

They've become very good with those things. They have done medical runs for emergencies; they've done dental search trips and found help. They've protected us from any kind of problems. We've never had any serious problem in the tsam. They protect us from ourselves sometimes when we ask for something they write back and say, "Are you supposed to have that?" [laughs, and laughing from re-treaters].

And so the caretakers and the people who help them have really done what they said they would do. It's so rare in the world; they've done much more than they every agreed to. When we're in deep retreat, some of us don't even go out to the toilet. We deliver them pee pee and poo poo in the food box and they take it and dispose of that, even those things they do. In addition to doing their own practice every day, I know, at least two hours [laughing]. They are rotating into deep re-treat themselves, and I hope they will keep that strictly.

There are other people who said they would take care of all the administrative problems, and they did, quietly and effectively. They moved here, and other people came with them to help.

The owners of this property said we could use it, and that they would be quiet. And they and the rancher who runs the cattle here have been perfect in their respect of the land, and isolation and quiet. We haven't had any disruptions at all. Oc-casionally there are motorcycles on the national park land [laughs], but they don't come in. After you've meditated for a month, they sound like the end of the world.

Other people said, "Oh, I'll come to Arizona and burn myself in the sun and build your yurts and places to stay," and they actually did it. A big group of people came. They didn't know much about carpentry or yurts, and they didn't expect the heat and then a snowstorm in the middle of it. But they came and they did it, beautiful work, we have beautiful places to stay. They actually did what they said they would do.

Other people got excited and said, "I'll send so many dollars of my pay to help with the expenses." Some people said, "I will give you my retirement fund." Other people said, "I will sell my house." People did [long pause]. People really did those things[long pause]. And so thank all those people.

People said, "I'll drive across the country in a truck with your stuff." And they really did it. They got lost in Texas [laughing], but they reached here. People from Mongolia said, "I'll send yurts, I'll find a freighter from China," and they did it. So I think we all have to be happy. Other people said, "I'll send you little packages, anonymous packages with things you need," and they did. They come. We'll know it's Christmas when, well it's against the rule, but when certain cookies arrive from a certain California coastal city [laughing]. Anyway everyone has done what they said, and it's wonderful and I think we should all be very happy.

OK, back to work.

We started with a teaching from Jesus. He said, "There be some people standing here who shall not taste of death before they see the kingdom." And then in Hindu tradition it's called *jivan mukti*, freedom before you die. In the Buddhist tradition, it's called *lu ma pangpar dakpa kachu du drowa*. Before you give up this body to enter heaven, the kingdom of heaven. In Tibetan, this kingdom is called *chi dakpa kachu, nang gye dakpa kachu*, outer heaven, and the inner heaven.

Then we talked about the choice, which is simple: gradual aging, gradual loss of all that you love, gradual loss of everything you've worked for and eventually to die. We talked about how reaching heaven in this life before you die satisfies the deepest urge of the human spirit, which is to do something of value for all other living things around you. We said that you can't ever be merely happy or content or satisfied with anything lesser than that.

The big question is, is there really any way that you can accomplish this goal? And then we started to talk about the goal itself. Two parts: outer heaven comes first, inner heaven comes second. They don't refer so much to outside you and inside you. We said that the outer heaven is like entering a training ground filled with holy beings, who help you to reach the inner kingdom.

We talked about an old argument in Tibet. Some holy beings said the outer heaven is a separate place, but other holy beings insisted it was the place where you are now, but different, transformed. In the end it's the same thing.

Then we spoke about the need to decide to meet your unavoidable destiny. You will never be satisfied, truly, until you become a being who can help in a single day millions of other beings, by a certain miracle of the very nature of existence. You will be the one person here who leads every other living creature to ultimate comfort and happiness by the nature of things. It seems impossible. Today we have to talk about why it's not.

To begin this work, you must find a good teacher who fits you. Teachers are like gloves, everybody needs a different size, everyone needs a different color and kind, and you have to find the gloves that fit you. Then work hard, surrender to this teacher and work very hard at what they tell you to do.

I saw a funny expression; it was, "Break your head at the feet of your master." It means it's not easy; they are pulling you faster than you are used to, and sometimes it hurts a little. But it's like that in these things. Any good teacher is tough. This is the same in piano and sports, and religion.

Then we spoke about the country that lies just outside the kingdom called *samadhi*. *Samadhi* is a state of continuous focus, peacefulness of mind, freedom from worry or possessiveness or anger or hatred. It rides smoothly throughout the day, focused on the present moment and living it fully. It's a state of heightened awareness that most of us only have, for example, when you're reading a very good book and you lose yourself in the book or listening to a very favorite song and lose yourself in the song.

Imagine being in that state of deep awareness all day. This is samadhi. We said samadhi is important in your meditation time, and samadhi is important as you go through your day at work or with your family, and at other times. Samadhi is like a blanket that covers the events of the whole day. Events start and end. Samadhi flows.

Then we talked about the things that help you reach samadhi. The first one we talked about was freeing your mind from things and learning to be a soldier in the war against possessions. They will sneak into your house. They will find many different ways to cling to you, and you have to brush them away. Be aggressive.

46

Each additional possession you have, whether it is an object, like a car, or another chair or another pair of shoes, each object detracts from your samadhi. It takes a certain amount of your mind to catalog it: to think about dusting it, to think about how to get rid of it, to think about whether you should move it today or not.

All of this prevents you from your destiny. You can't think straight with too many things. Have the things you need to live quietly, simply, cleanly, in an orderly way. And do the same with your relations with other people. Try to find around you people, whether they are beautiful, handsome, or not, it doesn't matter. Look for people who have the qualities of a good person who's living a good life. Try to limit your relationships to a few deep holy relationships with those people and don't make a jumble of your social life like your closet.

Then we spoke about this holy body, which we have been granted by our parents, and which was fed and clothed and raised up only through their constant moment-to-moment tireless efforts. It has this beautiful capacity to see the world, to taste things and feel things. Don't abuse this precious body. Don't hurt it with too much food, or wrong kinds of food. Don't subject it to extremes in your behavior that would hurt your body and hurt your mind, whether it's with the search for the things you need to live, or physical relationships.

Other things, like newspapers and magazines, don't overload this poor body and mind with them. Don't pile all the weight of all these possessions and stimulation and food on this poor body. It will die soon enough; you don't have to push it. Take care; it's a precious vehicle to use.

Then we spoke about two attitudes that take you into the outer kingdom. The first one has many complicated, technical names in Buddhist philosophy. We'll try *gyurpa te gyurpa* and *dak shen nyamje*, exchanging yourself with others, thinking about others. It boils down to common consideration of others around you. This is a very powerful cause to reach *samadhi*.

It's very simple, be considerate of others. Think of others' needs and wants before you do something. Constantly go through life without a ripple. Pass through other people's days quietly, gently, in a way that pleases them—only, of course, if it is moral. But within your power and within what's right, make people happy around you. Make them pleased by your passage through their day. Think of what they need and want.

47

Secondly, and maybe most importantly for entering the outer kingdom, free yourself from the poison of judging other people. People are like huge bubbles. They have experienced life for many years before you met them. Your bubble bumps into their bubble, you meet them for a few minutes or days, and we tend on that basis to assume that we know what they are. You have no idea what anyone else is, if you can't read their mind. You have no clue really why they do what they do. You have no idea what happened to them this morning in their home or in their meditation.

Free your mind from the poison of assuming that you know why they are doing what they do. There's no guarantee at all that they are not a divine being struggling to help you and you're fighting back ignorantly, like a small lizard stuck on tape.

That doesn't mean you shouldn't resist evil; you have to, but never assume that you know everything that's going on. Resist evil without adding the evil of assuming you know exactly what the other person's doing. Ultimately, there's no evil in your lifetime which has not come to you because you yourself have a seed of this evil in *you*, which *you* put there in the past. You can't see something wrong or bad without a seed of that same thing in you.

This is a curse and this is a blessing. It's a curse, because normally when we see a bad person, we blame them. We don't understand that the very reality of their existence is posited on our own perceptions. Someone loves them, someone thinks they are wonderful. You see them as bad because you have done something bad before, which put a seed in your mind to see them a certain way. No one is good, no one is bad; they only seem this way by different people because of the seeds in their own minds put there often by thinking someone is bad [*laughs*]. So be like the monkeys.

This brings us conveniently to the last teaching, which is how to enter the inner kingdom. I can think of two examples of ultimate reality or emptiness. The inner kingdom is deeply involved with ultimate reality, otherwise known as emptiness.

Emptiness is not—and never think it means—that nothing means anything. It's the opposite of that. Emptiness doesn't mean nothing exists. Emptiness doesn't mean nothing matters. It is the opposite of that. How? For example, when a person yells at you at work, there is probably someone else in the company who would see it as a very joyful event. Maybe they think that you deserve it, and they're happy that the boss agrees. Then you certainly feel otherwise—you feel the boss is being unreasonable.

So is the boss unreasonable or is the boss a good person who is trying to straighten out an employee? Of course you have to say it only depends on who's looking. This is the emptiness of the boss. The boss is neutral. If you have seeds in your mind to see him as wrathful, you will. If you have seeds in your mind to see him as kind, you will. He's neutral. Emptiness means neutral.

There's a deeper kind of emptiness. There's evidence for it everywhere. I will try to describe one. Buddhism speaks often of impermanence, that things are always changing and life is short. The very birth of a thing assures its destruction. No outer factor or influence is needed to destroy anything once it's born. Its very birth assures its destruction. This goes for worlds and people.

But there's a deeper impermanence. Things are changing moment by moment. Things are instant-by-instant changing. How long do they last before the next change? Some people say a certain number of divisions of a finger snap. It's not true. In an instant, a thing has changed more than once. The thing in the first half of the instant was closer to the start and the thing in the second half of the instant was closer to the end of the instant. Clearly there are two separate things. Within the instant, the thing has changed. The thing at the beginning of the instant is not the same as the thing at the end of the instant.

This is irrefutable. This is clear. We just don't think about it. Within a half an instant, the thing at the beginning of the half an instant is closer to the beginning than the thing at the end of the half an instant. It's clear that things last less than half an instant, because there's this distinction. A change has occurred in the first half an instant.

You know where this is leading. You can't find an object which is not in a state of change. There are no objects. It's impossible that you and I are seeing the first half of anything, because that has its own half. Something's screwy about reality. You just don't think about it. You can't be seeing the things you see the way you think you do. Objects don't come into your life and leave ten minutes later, after infinite changes. You wouldn't be able to see them.

Impermanence is a very frightening thing in one way. You can't be seeing the

49

things you see. So how are you seeing them? They aren't passing through your life, your mind is changing. Your mind takes hints of object and stitches together, glues together a convenient image and presents it to you and says, "This is a doughnut; this is a cookie." It can't be outside; it's impossible. Your mind is presenting an image to you and you chew on it. It makes you full.

This is the second important principle of empty things. They work. Of course they work. If you eat five or ten cookies, which retreatants in sort of a meditative overdose have been known to do, you quickly get sick, and start shaking all over.

They work, it's undeniable. You can't say cookies don't work. They are an image presented to your mind and therefore they work. The things you thought were real, the things you thought existed outside of you could never work the way you thought. A thing which changes in half the time it takes you to see could never be seen by you. Of course they don't exist the way you thought. Your mind is taking hints of objects and putting together an object and presenting it to your mind, and you bite into it and it's real.

Why bother with all this? If a doughnut works, why question a doughnut? Because it has everything to do with your fulfilling the reason why you were born. You didn't come here to eat, sleep, work hard, and then watch it all melt away. This is not a life. You know that. Because things are empty, because the world around you is empty, you have a chance to reach heaven.

How? When you see a person as bad, it is because you have been bad to someone else in the past. An imprint was put into your mind when you said "stupid," and that imprint takes time. It ripens, and then you meet a group of colors and sounds and it yells at you, "stupid employee."

The perception is coming from you, so you know where this is going. If you could clean your mind of any kind of negative thoughts, the worst of which is judging others; if you could look kindly upon others, knowing that something special may be going on that you aren't totally aware of. If you could do that, most of the bad seeds in your mind would be removed.

It's frightening to know that the world which you see around you is an absolutely perfect reflection of the condition of your own soul and heart. You can't see death; you can't see sickness among others or yourself, unless you have a seed for it from having harmed others in the past. So it's clear that there are some standing here who shall not taste of death before they see the kingdom.

There's a moving incident in the Bible. Jesus is in a synagogue. He's looking down at a paralyzed man, and the man says, "Please heal me. Please say 'walk.'"

And he says, "Think of the negative things you've done. Think of things you've done to hurt others, and regret them. Clean them from your mind. I say they should be cleaned now."

Then the people standing there got angry. "Who can clean these things? Why do you claim to have the authority or power to clean a person's mind, or to tell them to be clean?" He says, "How do you expect him to walk?"

It means even something as apparently irreversible as a paralyzed person or death itself can be changed if you change the seeds in your mind to see that thing. This is how you can overcome death itself in this life. It's clear; it's not difficult. It's proven by the thing about the boss. It's the real way to reach heaven, and there's no reason why you and I can't do it.

Gang la tongpa nyi rungwa de la tamche rungwa yin. Arya Nagarjuna, the great Buddhist from about two thousand years ago, said that all things are possible in the realm of emptiness. Jesus said that generally speaking, it's impossible to enter heaven, but all things are possible if you believe. Believe what? Just think, "OK, I believe?" Not like that.

It is understanding that, in the realm of emptiness, all things are possible. Nothing is impossible—not even stopping your death. Not even. Because of emptiness, you personally will become a being who helps countless other beings. Emptiness allows you to do it.

Emptiness is like sound itself. Because of sound, you can play the ultimate song. Emptiness is like the air itself. Because of the air, your song will be heard. Emptiness is like the ocean. Because of the ocean, the waves can move across it. You will move across the face of emptiness. You will reach millions of beings at once. How? I'll make a short demonstration, then we'll take a break. Then I'll say how.

[*Holds up sword.*] This beautiful holy sword was crafted in Ireland, in the holy

51

Ireland by very dear angelic friends, for this teaching. We'll do a meditation.

Just before you enter the inner kingdom, certain things happen within your being on an apocalyptic level. In this meditation, you should try to imagine your body as a light blue color. Not an object colored blue, but blueness itself. I can think of the sky, or if you've ever scuba dived, looking up from very clean water blue. The blue is almost fluorescent, or the blue is blueness. It's a light blue. Not a bright light, just sort of like water or crystal blue, and you imagine that inside your whole body is like that.

Then coming down the axis of your body is a straight ray of golden light. Like if you've ever been under water and looked up and seen the sunlight pierce the water. In this meditation, picture the inside of yourself, with no hard stomach or ribs, just this beautiful crystal blue and then a shaft of golden light coming down your body just in front of your back bone so it comes down straight from the tip of your head down. Tracing your back in front of the backbone and coming down to the level of your navel, your belly button. So, let's try that first.

Close your eyes, take a few deep breaths, and imagine your body is not made of blood and guts anymore; it's like the blue part of a rainbow inside. Then see the ray of golden light, a shaft of soft golden light, piercing the blue from the middle of the top of your head, down to the level of your navel, running along in a very straight line just in front of where your backbone used to be.

Now imagine that you can be inside that shaft of light, and you can hear something like the high voices of a choir. Then you look down, and you see this sword that I am holding. The cross that is formed by the handle and the blade is at your navel, the handle goes down a little farther, and the blade pierces the golden shaft. The blade runs up your back, inside.

The tip touches your heart—not your physical heart, but the place in that shaft which is across from your heart. The blade is clear like diamond. The tip of the blade begins to get hot. It glows red like steel heated to incandescent red. Great showers, great streams of red light flow, burst forth from the tip of the sword. They penetrate your skin, and they pass out into the air, great shafts of poles of light red beautiful light in all directions.

People living on countless planets look up in the night sky. There's a new star; it's red. Somehow they know it means that a special being has been born. That being is you. And on every planet where people look up and see this red star you will come to bring them teaching and teach them how not to taste of death.

Okay, we'll take a break. Mr. John Brady should come and pass the sword around, and everyone should try now or later to hold it. Remember, it takes a good Irishman to pass this sword around. Take a break.

[Break]

I'll try to finish quickly, I know it is getting cold and also I suspect that people have to travel.

When I think of Emptiness, I like to think of a huge block of ice on the desert ground, between me and the Dragoon Mountains. We often dream about the sea and ice cream—I don't know why. But imagine walking up to this huge block of ice or diamond, the size of a city block, high as a building, and in it you can see your reflection. It is like a mirror.

That is what Emptiness does; it allows objects a place to be. Even if those objects are reflections of your own mind, they work. The world works; it is not unreal. A car will break your legs; a cookie will fill your stomach. You are seeing the car break your legs, because you hurt someone in the past. The seed of hurting someone is ripening in your mind and organizing otherwise random colors and shapes into a steel bumper, and it's real.

The funny thing about this mirror is that it doesn't reflect you immediately. You make a funny face in the mirror, grrrah! and about six months later it reflects back this ugly guy. You've forgotten it's a mirror, and you get angry at this ugly person, and then you plant another seed and you make another face and six months later there's two ugly guys in your life.

This is true. This is the way to heaven. This is the key.

Your being has four parts. There's the world you live in right now: you are experiencing a desert getting colder. And then there's the second level of your gross physical body, the skin and bones and blood.

Then there are two levels, which are hard to see. There's an inner core of your being. It's a very subtle pipeline, like that shaft of golden light which runs up and down your body near the backbone. Within this shaft run energies, called wind in Tibetan, and they run linked to your thoughts. When you have a clean happy pure thought, when you make a conscious deliberate effort to see something good in a person you don't like, then the energies linked to your thought run up and down this channel smoothly.

Then you have an innermost core at the very center of your being. It's usually associated with the heart, or in that shaft at the level of your heart. Within this inner most core is the capacity to experience emptiness directly.

There's a beautiful interplay happening. When you have a pure thought, the energies linked to your thoughts are loosened to run as they should. This creates a parallel goodness in your external body. You actually get healthier. Your body is stronger, lighter, and you have health.

And there's another parallel event in the outer world—you begin to see things more pure and beautiful. Just having a single charitable thought about a person who bothers you sets off sympathetic events in your body, in the core of your being, and a parallel goodness in the outer world around you.

But there's a time delay; it takes time for the outer parallel events to happen, unless you understand what's happening. Unless you understand that everything is a reflection of your mind; unless you understand clearly that when you meet a person who seems bad, they only seem bad because of a seed in your own mind.

With this knowledge, knowledge itself of the emptiness or blankness of that person, they become neutral—they are only colors and shapes and sounds. Your mind weaves that into a person yelling at you, because you yelled at someone before.

If you clearly understand this highest truth, then that time lag becomes shorter and shorter and shorter. There comes a time when, if your thoughts are exceptionally pure, then your body begins to change before your eyes, and a parallel event is occurring in the world around you.

If your mind becomes exceptionally pure because you understand why things happen, your body begins to change into light. The world around you, which has

54

always been a delayed reflection of your thoughts and deeds, each rewarded according to his deeds, then the world itself begins to transform. You can actually watch it happen.

At the final stage of this process, your being begins to reflect the innermost core. Meaning you become the huge block of diamond, as well as the most exquisite creature reflected in its surface. You are at the same time the ultimate reality of all things, and you are the most precious, faultless, absolutely pure being whose image is in that.

Because that truth extends to all places, you are now reflected in all worlds. Everyone living anywhere in this huge galaxy universe of ours would be able to see you. You would appear to anyone who needed you, and you would appear to them in the way that helped them the most.

I want to repeat it one time, because it is not very clear sometimes. You have four parts of your being: the outer world, a desert growing much colder. And you have a body. And you are seeing these two things, the way you see them as something cold, or mortal, because of thoughts you planted in your own mind.

You have to clean those thoughts and seeds from your mind. It's important, very important, to say that only you can clean them. If someone else could clean them you wouldn't be here. The best way to clean them is to stop repeating them.

If you have been judging others, and I have through my whole life, from hour to hour, hundreds of times a day—in little ways, not evil—then if you decide to stop, if you try hard the next time you feel hurt by someone or irritated by someone, if you consciously try to see the good in them and stop looking at the bad, it creates more seeds to see good.

Everyone has pureness in them; you just aren't looking. Then if you honestly try, the old seeds in your mind will be destroyed. You have the capacity, therefore, to make your mind pure. As the mind becomes pure, the thoughts running in the core of your being gain freedom to move properly. This causes the inner energies or winds of your body to flow properly.

A parallel event happens in your outer body—you get stronger, healthier, younger. Eventually the body itself changes into light, because your mind is forcing you to see it like that, therefore it *is* light. And then a parallel event is triggered in your world outside; and you are living in a place of perfect beauty.

When this reaches its final culmination, you actually begin to relate with the innermost drop or being of purity, and part of you becomes the foundation—that thing which is the foundation of all being, which is emptiness. Because you have become that, you appear wherever that emptiness reaches, and it reaches all places. And so everyone can see you.

You come into those worlds as a holy, ultimately holy being, born, appearing on that planet, teaching each person, and then your teachings spread more and more. And you become like the Buddha or the Jesus of that world, and of countless worlds like that.

This is your destiny; this is what each human being, what every being will become. You know it in your heart; you want to do it in your heart.

I would like to end with another incident. Jesus is standing in a temple, being questioned by a group of scholars. He's a carpenter; he doesn't know much. When he goes back to his hometown to teach, they throw him out of the temple; they drag him up to a mountain; and they try to kill him; they try to throw him off a cliff.

But he stands before the scholars and he answers honestly from his heart, and people are stunned by his answers. One of the scholars is moved and says, "I have a question. I honestly want to know the answer from you. I think you can answer it; I have seen you answer the others from your heart so truly."

And Jesus says, "What?"

And the scholar says, "What is the highest teaching of all?"

Then Jesus says, "First is to devote your whole heart and mind and life to the search for heaven. And the second is like unto it; treat other people exactly as you would treat yourself—spend the same effort to make them happy that you would spend to make yourself happy."

The man is struck. He says, "This is more truth than I've ever heard before."

Jesus says to him, "You are close to the kingdom."

We miss each of you very much. And we were a little afraid to start such a long retreat, fearing that some of you might be hurt or might not be there when we finished. So I think on behalf of all of the people here in retreat and others who are helping, we ask each of you to take good care of yourselves and practice well and try to follow good teachings, be happy. But most of all try to promise us to be here when we finish because we miss you so much and love you so much. Thank you.

Verses:

To the Inner Kingdom

I.

There be some standing here
Which shall not taste of death
Till they see the kingdom;
Jivan mukti, lu ma pangpar,
But how?

The choice is those you love
Ripped away, over the edge.
One house crumbles,
The other is sold.
The empty feeling of the unfulfilled,
Monotony to the grave.

You were not meant to lie within the egg;
Pierce the shell,
See the world in color,
Fly to the empty sky.

Great Garuda,
Guardian of the children of the stars -
You will never be happy until this moment.

Now turn and see
Who put you here.

II.

The kingdoms are two,
Inner and outer,
Come to the outer,
And then to the inner.

The outer is the apprentice song
The inner the air that carries it.

Both depend upon the fact
That nothing exists from its own side.

Make one decision,
Seek and learn
From friend and friends,
Hidden gems of the earth.

Samadhi is a state of grace
That borders on the Kingdom

Samadhi before the altar,
Samadhi before the world.

If you would be perfect,
Fight the good war
Against things:
Those that move and those that don't,
Advance guard and troops in the trenches.

Break the tyranny
Of the senses;
The devil is not gone,
Gone to the refrigerator,
The closet, the bed, the paper.

Behind the glass,
Behind the desk.
Seek first for the kingdom.

III.

Whatsoever you would,
Move through lives
Without a ripple.

If you're not like him,
Judge not, for you will:
A plank and a piece of dust,
A mountain under forest,
For they are your perfect reflection.

Only a bubble
Touching a bubble;
Desert creatures
Fighting life
And granting it.
People and events

Live like the three,
Resist evil
First at the source;
But be gentle there as well.

Silence and a single point
Shifting throughout the day;
Hours on the cushion—
The outer kingdom's come.

IV.

To learn to play
The final song
You must become then
Sound itself:
Enter the inner kingdom.

The breath, the wind, the inner wind
Moving in reflection
Of heart and understanding,
Key to the realm of emptiness,
Key to the impossible
Possible for heaven,
For in this realm believing
Becomes reality.

Nothing greater than these two;
You have spoken true, and you
Are not far from the Kingdom.

Acknowledgements

A big thank you to all the people who helped make the three-year retreat and these teachings happen.

To the retreatants Geshe Michael Roach, Lama Christie McNally, Lama Thubten Pelma, Lama Trisangma Watson, Lama Ora Maimes, and Ven Tenzin Chogkyi, thank you for inspiring us all and dedicating your lives to serve others.

It could not have happened without the caretakers. Thank you to Ven. Jigme Palmo (Elly van der Pas), Amber Moore and Ven Lobsang Chukyi (Anne Lindsey); Brian Pearson, Sarah Laitinen, Sid Johnson, Keith Nevin, Ven. Gyelse (Gail Deutsch), Mercedes Bahleda, and Deb Bye, who helped with everything.

And to Winston and Andrea McCullough, the directors of Diamond Mountain, and their wonderful children; Ted and Andrea Lemon, who shared their home; David and Susan Stumpf and everyone else who helped with construction; the 400 sponsors who helped pay the bills, and the 187 people who came to the teachings; our lamas and teachers Khen Rinpoche Geshe Lobsang Tharchin, Geshe Thubten Rinchen, Lama Zopa Rinpoche, Sir Gene Smith, Sharon Gannon, David Life, David Swenson, Lady Ruth Lauer, and Laura Donnelly; Jerry and Marjorie Dixon, who let us use their land; John Brady, John Stillwell, Salim Lee, and the many many secret angels, (you know who you are) who keep pretending that you are normal people.

The Quiet Retreat Teaching books were brought into the world by the work of many hands. Ven. Jigme Palmo of Diamond Mountain University Press morphed the teachings into book form. Special thanks for layout and cover design to Katey Fetchenhier. DMU-Press intern Michelle Ross was a huge help with printing logistics. Thank you for endless hours of proof-reading to Joel Crawford, Michela Wilson, Kelly Fetchenhier, Janice Sanders, Karlie Sanders, Cassie Heinle, Lindsay Nelson, and Michelle Ross. Big thank you to Marc Ross for spending his precious free hours making manuscript corrections. We would especially like to express boundless appreciation to Ven. Jigme Palmo for her uncanny ability to do 10 things at once—and do them all well.

And of course, our infinite gratitude to our Teacher, Geshe Michael Roach, without whom these extraordinary teachings would not exist.

CPSIA information can be obtained
at www.ICGtesting.com
Printed in the USA
LVOW11s1240071017

551392LV00003BA/436/P